CHURCH MUSIC SOCIETY PUBLICATION: 023A
Hon. General Editor: Richard Lyne

CO_____ COPY

for the Choir and Congregation of St. Mary's Church, No

Saint Mary's Mass

Music by ANTHONY CÆSAR

Kyrie

Alternative version of Kyrie

Gloria

Glo-ry to God in the high-est, and peace to his peo-ple on earth. — Lord God, hea-ven-ly King, al--migh-ty God — and Fa - ther, we wor - ship you, we give — you thanks, we praise — you — for your glo - ry. Lord — Je - sus Christ, on - ly Son of the Fa - ther, Lord God, Lamb of God, you take a - way the sin — of the world: have mer - cy on us: you are seat - ed at the right hand of the Fa - ther: re - ceive —— our prayer.

Tempo primo

3

Gospel Responses

Sanctus – Benedictus

Acclamations

Agnus Dei

Acknowledgment

The *Gloria*, the *Sanctus*, the *Benedictus* and the *Agnus Dei* from *The Order for Holy Communion Rite A* from the Alternative Service Book 1980 are © International Consultation on English Texts and are reproduced with permission of the Central Board of Finance of the Church of England.

ISBN 0-19-395363-3

Origination by Jeanne Fisher, Ludlow, Shropshire
Printed by Halstan & Co. Ltd., Amersham, Bucks

Pack of 10 copies
Not available separately

9 780193 953635